The Career Renaissance

A Woman's Guide to Career Transformation

DR. TITA L. GRAY

San Diego, CA

Published by

Montezuma Publishing
Aztec Shops Ltd.
San Diego State University
San Diego, California 92182-1701

619-594-7552

www.montezumapublishing.com

Copyright © 2023

All Rights Reserved.

ISBN: 978-1-7269-0860-3

Copyright © 2023 by Montezuma Publishing and the author Tita L. Gray. The compilation, formatting, printing and binding of this work is the exclusive copyright of Montezuma Publishing and the author Tita L. Gray. All rights reserved. No part of this work may be reproduced, stored in a retrieval system, or transmitted in any form or by any means, including digital, except as may be expressly permitted by the applicable copyright statutes or with written permission of the Publisher or Author(s).

Publishing Manager: Lia Dearborn

Production Manager: Steve Murawka

Design and Layout: Lia Dearborn and Tita L. Gray

Cover Design: Lia Dearborn

Contents

Acknowledgment v
Introduction 1

One
    The Effects of Fear 7

Two
    The Importance of Purpose 11

Three
    Career Transition Challenges 15

Four
    Career Preparation 21
        Ten Steps 21

Five
    Career Preparation for Entrepreneurs 27

Six
    Self-Awareness 31

Seven
    Skills & Ability Development 37

Eight
    Your Network 41

Nine
    Flexibility & Adaptability 45

Ten
    Habits 47

Eleven
    Culture 51

Twelve
- Resources 55
  - Websites for Success 55
  - Career Inspiration TED Talks 55
  - Motivational TED Talks 57
  - Podcasts 57
  - Suggested Reading 59
  - Blogs 60

Thirteen
- Top Industries 61
  - Alphabetical Listing of Industries 62

Fourteen
- Conclusion 67

Acknowledgment

My mom transitioned to heaven on December 26, 2022. She was my inspiration always to do my best, be my best, and treat everyone respectfully. She was also my inspiration to write this book to give back for everything I have gained and learned. My life and career have always been focused on or engaged in helping others.

Including my mom and grandma, this book is for all of the fantastic women I learned from, that gave me opportunities and encouragement and told me the truth no matter how much it hurt. Always find quiet moments for reflection, manifestation, and cleansing of your spiritual closets. You are enough and a unique blessing just as you are. Your path is drawn, and although you may face obstacles, they are only tests of your resilience, faith, and patience. I wish you love, abundance, and peace in your journey.

Much Love,
Dr. Tita Gray

The Career Renaissance

Introduction

AWAKENING

I walked a path of uncertainty
my steps were filled with trepidation,
my purpose contained,
when I looked around for those who told me I
wouldn't, shouldn't, and couldn't; they were no longer
there, only a reflection of myself still following a dream
that wasn't mine.

Dr. Tita Gray

Women, you are more powerful and resourceful than you know. As a seasoned career coach, author, executive, and woman of color that has faced adversity due to ethnicity and lack of preparation time and time again, I can tell you that reaching your career milestones can be achieved. The main thing that you must focus on is the journey, not the destination. The journey contains gems like your stories, experiences, pain, triumphs, and memories. Your purpose in life can stretch far beyond your wildest dreams; all you have to do is believe in the impossible becoming possible. I have worked in several industries, but overall, academia gave me meaning and a sense of purpose, and due to a lack of self-awareness, it took me twenty years professionally to find it.

A career renaissance refers to a significant period of reinvention, renewal, and transformation in one's professional life. It represents a profound shift or revival in your career trajectory, often characterized by a direction, purpose, or fulfillment change. The concept of a career renaissance encompasses several vital elements. A career renaissance involves reinventing and reviving oneself professionally. It may entail changing industry, job function, or even starting a business. It goes beyond minor adjustments or incremental growth and encompasses a more substantial transformation. You often experience a renewed sense of purpose and passion during a career renaissance in your work. You may reassess your values, interests, and goals, seeking alignment and meaning in your career choices. A career renaissance often involves significant growth and development. It may entail acquiring new skills, expanding knowledge, or pursuing further education or training to excel in the chosen path.

Career Renaissance welcomes change as an opportunity rather than a challenge. It requires you to embrace uncertainty, step out of your comfort zones, and adapt to new environments or industries. It often involves taking calculated risks and being open to new experiences. It aims to increase satisfaction and fulfillment in one's professional life. It emphasizes finding work that aligns with personal values, utilizing strengths, and creating a sense of joy and accomplishment. *A career renaissance is not limited by age, as it can occur at any stage of one's professional journey.* It can be sparked by personal growth, a shift in priorities, or a desire for greater fulfillment. It is a time of self-reflection, exploration and intentional decision-making to shape a more purposeful and satisfying career path.

Ultimately, a career renaissance represents a transformative phase where you can redefine your professional identity, pursue your passions, and create a more meaningful and rewarding work life. Mary Barra is the CEO of General Motors (GM) and has become a prominent figure in the automotive industry. She experienced a career renaissance when transitioning from engineering to leadership positions within GM. Barra's career journey showcases the power of embracing new challenges, developing new skills, and rising to top executive positions.

This book is for you if you need assistance with reinventing yourself or facing fears or doubts in deciding on a career direction. For many women, the fear of starting over is debilitating, stressful, and instilled with insecurity. I didn't write this book to sugarcoat anything. There are grave and legitimate reasons why you are in a situation that is not necessarily true to your purpose or where you want to be. Going through a career transformation can be highly stressful, and sometimes take months or years to find your calling and how to pursue it. During career exploration, it is essential to have the support of your loved ones or friends; however, your decisions need to be based on your *understanding of who you are and what you need.* Career dreams begin long before you are an adult, and it is influenced, and even at times dictated, by family, friends, and mentors.

We often make choices based on what other people believe is suitable for us; however, complete reliance on others complicates the process of relationships because it is only possible to please some. The key is to purposefully and knowledgeably articulate your career decisions. That starts with having an understanding of *yourself and facing your fears*. In our life journey, we will not always make decisions that are a good fit or seemingly suitable for us at the time. We often make decisions based on the choices, options, and information present at the time, and in hindsight, we realize that they were not always the best decisions. Regardless of the outcome of your career choice, being self-aware and self-reliant are critical to how you adapt and navigate your career transition. Instead of punishing yourself for the past and regardless of the circumstances, turn that path into a story of survival.

The central premise of this book is to help you overcome any barriers that fear has placed on you, assist you in finding your purpose, and encourage you to be intentional with your career journey. It is to encourage and reignite the dreams that are planted in you. Many of us have a dream, hobby, or something we love, and it can tell us a lot about ourselves and our aspirations. For example, I have never considered myself a writer but have always loved words. I love the meaning and the sound; I like how they can connect a story or add emphasis. Not surprising, then, that writing poetry and stories always provided me with a lot of comfort and reflection. It was my source of self-awareness, self-actualization, and connection.

The intent of this book is for you to pay more attention to YOU and what has always brought you a sense of joy and connection. It is for you to look at life through a different lens, one that is more holistic and close to your heart. Time, knowledge, and purpose are precious and should not be wasted or taken for granted because of fear. They are the foundation of what shapes a meaningful career. This book encourages you to think differently about how you approach career decision-making and abolish the crippling effects of fear.

When you land in an industry you feel a strong connection with; you can begin to actualize the vast opportunities ahead of you. You can see yourself rising as an executive or an entrepreneur in that field. You can see yourself making a difference and continuing your education to further your career trajectory. A job and a career are two distinct concepts that refer to different aspects of employment. A job is typically a specific position or role an individual performs to earn income. It is often temporary or short-term and focuses primarily on fulfilling immediate financial needs. Jobs can vary in terms of skill level, responsibility, and duration. People may hold multiple jobs throughout their working lives.

Job satisfaction may come from compensation, work-life balance, and the immediate tasks performed. Conversely, a career refers to a long-term professional journey that spans multiple jobs and often involves progression, development, and the pursuit of personal and professional goals. Unlike a career, a career focuses more on a broader trajectory and requires planning, skill development, and strategic decision-making. It involves building expertise, gaining experience, and often pursuing advancement opportunities within a specific field or industry. Career satisfaction may come from personal growth, fulfillment, achievement of long-term goals, and alignment with one's values and passions. There are critical differences between a job and a career. A job is often seen as a means to an end, primarily focused on financial stability.

Conversely, a career involves finding purpose and fulfillment by aligning work with personal values, interests, and long-term aspirations. A job may require specific skills, while a career involves continuous skill development and learning to advance professionally. Career progression often includes acquiring new skills, taking on more responsibilities, and seeking growth opportunities. A career involves strategic planning, goal setting, and envisioning a long-term path. It requires considering factors such as education, training, networking, and personal aspirations. A job may require a different level of planning and long-term goal setting.

It's important to note that a job can be a stepping stone to a career. Many start with a job to gain experience, earn income, and explore different industries or fields. Over time, you develop your skills, interests, and goals, eventually transitioning into a career that aligns with your long-term aspirations. Both jobs and careers are significant depending on your circumstances, priorities, and goals. Some of you may find job satisfaction by focusing on immediate needs and maintaining a work-life balance. In contrast, others may seek fulfillment through a long-term career journey that allows for growth, development, and achieving personal and professional milestones.

As a result of never giving up on my dreams and aspirations of being a professor and having friends and colleagues who believed in me, I began a career I had always longed for in education. That opportunity led to my appointment as an Assistant Dean, completing a doctorate and writing three books to give back to others everything that has been given to me. And now, I am on another journey because no matter the setbacks, I know how to follow my purpose without fear or doubt, and so can you.

Dr. Tita Gray

The Career Renaissance

One

The Effects of Fear

It is normal to feel fear. Fear is a powerful emotion that can create uncertainty and insecurity about the future. It can manifest in various forms, such as fear of rejection, fear of failure, fear of the unknown, fear of judgment or criticism, or fear of not meeting expectations. And yes, fear of pursuing career dreams and aspirations. When you are afraid, you may hesitate to take risks or step out of your comfort zones. You may worry about the potential consequences of pursuing new career plans, such as financial instability, social judgment, or the possibility of just not succeeding. These fears can hold you back from pursuing your goals and dreams.

Despite her massive success as a media mogul, Oprah Winfrey has openly discussed her fear of success. She has discussed the pressure and anxiety that came with her success and the fear of not living up to expectations. However, she recognized her fears and worked through them to become one of the most influential women in the world. Understandably, fear can also lead to self-doubt and a lack of confidence. You may question your abilities and fear that you need to be more skilled or competent to pursue your desired career path. Self-doubt can prevent you from taking the necessary steps to pursue your aspirations or even discourage you from exploring new opportunities. The renowned tennis player Serena Williams has faced fear and self-doubt throughout her career. Despite her numerous achievements and titles, she has openly expressed her fear of failure and the pressure to maintain her success. Nevertheless, she always pushed herself and achieved remarkable success in her sport.

Fear can be induced by external factors such as societal expectations, parental pressure, or the fear of disappointing others. These external pressures can further prevent you from following your true passions and instead push you towards more conventional or safer career choices. However, it's important to note that fear is a natural and shared emotion, and everyone experiences it to some degree. Overcoming fear and pursuing career aspirations require you to challenge your fears, develop resilience, and take calculated risks. Seeking support from mentors, building a solid support network, and cultivating self-belief can all help overcome fear and pursue one's career aspirations. These fears can create significant barriers and hold you back from taking the necessary risks and actions to pursue your career goals.

Fear of failure is a common obstacle that many people face. The fear of not succeeding or making mistakes can paralyze and prevent you from even pursuing your aspirations. The fear of judgment or criticism from others can also have a substantial impact, as you may worry about what others will think if you fail or if your chosen path is unconventional or poorly understood by others. Additionally, fear can arise from the discomfort of stepping out of one's comfort zone. Pursuing a career aspiration involves taking risks, making changes, and venturing into the unknown. These obstacles can be intimidating and create a fear of the unfamiliar, causing you to resist pursuing your aspirations and instead opt for the safety and familiarity of your current situation.

In the book *The 50th Law*, the author states that there are two ways of handling fear: passive and active. He shares that we avoid situations that cause anxiety in the passive mode. The active mode translates to temporary things that most of us face at some point in our lives, such as the death of someone close or something important not working out as we hoped. In this mode, when faced with a situation we feared, if or when it happens, we find the strength somehow to persevere. In the active mode, some people live in constant conflict or danger daily and must confront their fears repeatedly. For example, being on the frontlines of war, growing up in extreme poverty and crime, or going through repeated sexual assault. Many people do not overcome these circumstances, and their spirits are damaged by misfortune. What separates those that go under and those that rise above misfortune is the persistence and the strength of their will.

Nelson Mandela, the renowned South African anti-apartheid revolutionary and political leader, faced severe adversity during his fight against racial segregation. In 1964, he was sentenced to life imprisonment for his activism. Despite being confined to a small prison cell for 27 years, Mandela refused to let fear consume him. He dedicated himself to education, self-improvement, and maintaining his resolve for a democratic and equal South Africa. After his release in 1990, Mandela continued his fight, becoming the country's first black president and a symbol of hope and reconciliation. There are times when we have little control over our circumstances; however, there is one thing we do have control over our mindset. If we can overcome our trepidation and forge a fearless attitude toward adversity, we establish grit and determination as a way of life.

Maya Angelou, the illustrious poet, and civil rights activist, endured a traumatic childhood that left her voiceless for several years. At seven, she was sexually abused by her mother's boyfriend. Feeling responsible for his subsequent death, she stopped speaking for nearly five years, afraid that her words had caused the tragedy. However, she found relief through reading and writing poetry and began to heal. Maya Angelou eventually regained her voice and became a powerful advocate for equality and human rights, using her words to inspire and uplift others. Overcoming fear is a crucial step in pursuing career aspirations. It requires self-awareness, courage, and a willingness to confront and challenge those fears. Building confidence, setting realistic goals, seeking support from mentors or trusted individuals, and gradually exposing oneself to the situations that cause fear can all be helpful strategies in overcoming fear and moving forward toward career aspirations.

Adopting a growth mindset is crucial, which means viewing failures and setbacks as opportunities for learning and growth rather than personal shortcomings. Recognize that failures are part of the learning process and provide valuable lessons that can lead to future success. Embrace challenges and be open to new experiences. Remember, fear is a natural emotion that doesn't have to paralyze you. By understanding your fears, adopting a positive attitude, taking calculated risks, and seeking support, you can manage and overcome the fear of career failure, allowing yourself to pursue your goals with confidence and resilience. In addition to adopting a growth mindset, incorporating systems thinking habits is crucial, and I discuss that further in the habits chapter.

The Career Renaissance

Two

The Importance of Purpose

"Leaders must continually ask: is my work worthy of my sense of purpose, or just a means to an end?" — Sandy Shugart Ph.D.

Purpose plays a significant role in shaping and guiding our lives. It gives us a sense of direction, meaning, and motivation. The concept of purpose plays a significant role in our lives, providing direction, meaning, and motivation. Purpose provides a sense of fulfillment in life. When we have a clear purpose, we understand why we do what we do, which can bring a deep sense of satisfaction and contentment. Purpose gives our lives a more profound sense of meaning and fulfillment. It connects our actions and achievements to something larger than ourselves when we feel that what we do matters and contributes to a more significant cause; it brings a sense of satisfaction and contentment.

Steve Jobs, the co-founder of Apple Inc., was driven by a desire to create innovative products that would transform how people interact with technology. His relentless pursuit of excellence and attention to detail shaped the company's vision and led to groundbreaking products such as the iPhone, iPad, and Macintosh computers. Having a purpose ignites our motivation and drives us to pursue our goals and overcome obstacles. It provides a source of inspiration and resilience during challenging times. Having a clear sense of purpose gives us a reason to get up every morning and pursue our goals. It provides motivation, enthusiasm, and a sense of direction. We are more likely to persevere through challenges and setbacks when we have a purpose.

Purpose helps us set meaningful goals and make decisions aligned with our values and long-term vision. It serves as a compass, guiding us toward actions that align with our purpose and avoiding distractions or choices that may lead us astray. It is a guiding principle helping us prioritize our time, energy, and resources. When we have a clear purpose, we can make choices that harmonize with our long-term aspirations. Mother Teresa, a Catholic nun and missionary, dedicated her life to serving the poor and marginalized in India and worldwide. She founded the Missionaries of Charity, which provides care and support to those in need. Mother Teresa's selfless devotion to helping others made her an iconic figure of compassion and humanitarianism. Purpose helps us prioritize our time, energy, and resources. It enables us to focus on what truly matters to us, filter out distractions, and allocate our resources effectively to achieve our goals.

Research has shown that having a sense of purpose is linked to better physical and mental health. People with a strong sense of purpose often experience lower levels of stress, depression, and anxiety. Purpose provides a sense of direction and stability, promoting overall well-being. Pursuing purpose often involves self-reflection, self-discovery, and personal growth. It pushes us outside our comfort zones, challenges us to develop new skills, and allows us to explore our potential. Purpose allows us to make a positive impact on the world around us. When we align our actions with our purpose, we can contribute to causes that are meaningful to us, create change, and leave a lasting legacy. A purpose is linked to greater resilience and well-being. It provides a sense of identity and self-worth, fostering a positive outlook and reducing stress. People with a strong sense of purpose tend to be more resilient in facing adversity, as they can draw on their purpose to find meaning and strength. Jesse Owens, an African-American track and field athlete, competed in the 1936 Olympics held in Nazi Germany. He faced racial discrimination and intense pressure but found purpose in proving that excellence knows no boundaries. Owens won four gold medals, defying the Nazi ideology of Aryan supremacy. His achievements broke down racial barriers and inspired generations of athletes.

When we have a sense of purpose, it often involves contributing to the well-being of others or making a positive impact on the world around us. Pursuing our purpose can inspire and motivate others, fostering a sense of community and collective progress. Purpose helps us prioritize our efforts and focus on what truly matters. It acts as a compass, guiding us in the right direction and preventing us from getting lost or overwhelmed. With a clear purpose, we can avoid distractions and progress toward our desired outcomes. Dr. Martin

Two — The Importance of Purpose

Luther King Jr. was a prominent American civil rights movement leader. When Rosa Parks was arrested for refusing to give up her seat to a white passenger on a Montgomery city bus on December 1, 1955, King was a twenty-six-year-old minister just a year into his job at the Dexter Avenue Baptist Church in Montgomery, who imagined that he might one day become a professor. On December 5, a meeting was called, and held in the building of an African-American congregation, the Holt Street Baptist Church. That afternoon, the boycott organizers met in King's church basement and voted to call themselves the Montgomery Improvement Association. Then, to his surprise, and probably because he was not well known and no one else was eager to accept the risk of white reprisal, King was elected the group's president. It was after six o'clock. The mass meeting was scheduled for seven. King rushed home to tell his wife and to write a speech. He dedicated his career to fighting against racial discrimination and advocating for equality and justice for African Americans. King's iconic "I Have a Dream" speech inspires a generation.

Purpose adds depth and significance to our lives. It helps us find meaning, guides our decisions and actions, and contributes to our overall well-being and the well-being of others. Bethany Hamilton, a professional surfer, encountered a life-altering event at the age of 13 when she lost her left arm in a shark attack. Despite this traumatic experience, Hamilton found purpose in her love for surfing and faith. She refused to let her disability define her and returned to competitive surfing, inspiring many as she excelled in her sport. Furthermore, speaking of athletes finding purpose, Muhammad Ali, one of the greatest heavyweight boxers in history, faced numerous challenges inside and outside the ring. He was stripped of his boxing titles and faced backlash for his political views. Ali found purpose in standing up against racial inequality, war, and injustice. His resilience, charisma, and activism made him influential in the fight for civil rights.

In summary, the purpose is essential because it provides motivation and direction. It fuels our actions, fosters fulfillment, and enables us to make choices aligned with our values. Ultimately, having a sense of purpose contributes to our overall well-being and allows us to make a positive impact on ourselves and others.

The Career Renaissance

Three

Career Transition Challenges

Unlike men, women going through career transitions can face specific challenges due to societal, cultural, and organizational factors. Below are some challenges women commonly encounter during career transitions; see if any of these below apply to you. I will touch on each topic more in-depth throughout the book.

Women often face gender bias and stereotypes in the workplace, which can affect their career transitions. You may encounter assumptions about your abilities or limitations based on gender, which can hinder your progress or limit opportunities in your new field. Women's experiences are not solely defined by gender but are also shaped by the intersection of race, ethnicity, and other identities. Intersectionality recognizes that multiple dimensions of identity interact and can lead to unique experiences and challenges. The combination of gender and racial identity can compound the barriers and biases women face during career transitions. This area dramatically affects transgender women due to explicit and implicit bias.

Biases can also affect women with disabilities significantly. Battling disabilities that hinder career change can be challenging, but with determination, resilience, and the proper support, it is possible to overcome these obstacles. Start by deeply understanding your disabilities and how they may impact your career transition. Embrace self-acceptance and recognize that disabilities do not define your abilities or potential. Acknowledge your strengths and unique qualities that can contribute to your desired career path. Seek out disability support organizations, vocational rehabilitation services, or career counselors who specialize in assisting people with disabilities. These professionals can provide guidance, resources, and accommodations to help you navigate career challenges and make informed decisions.

It would be best to research companies and organizations committed to inclusivity and supporting employees with disabilities. Look for employers that prioritize accessibility, reasonable accommodations, and foster an inclusive work environment. Examine their policies, programs, and success stories of people with disabilities in their workforce.

Look for accessible learning options or accommodations that can support your learning process. Build a strong network of peers, mentors, and professionals who can offer guidance, support, and connections. Seek mentors who have successfully navigated career challenges related to disabilities and can provide insights and encouragement. One of the most critical points is to be proactive in advocating for your needs and reasonable accommodations in the workplace. Familiarize yourself with your rights under disability laws and regulations, and communicate your requirements effectively to employers or potential colleagues. Assertively articulate how accommodations enable you to contribute effectively in your desired role.

Recognize that facing obstacles and setbacks is a natural part of any career journey, especially when dealing with disabilities. Cultivate resilience, perseverance, and a positive mindset to navigate challenges. Seek support from a counselor or support group to help manage stress, maintain motivation, and cope with the emotional aspects of the journey. Remember, your disabilities do not define your worth or potential. Embrace your unique strengths, seek appropriate support, and leverage available resources to overcome obstacles and pursue a fulfilling career path aligned with your abilities and aspirations.

Balancing work and personal responsibilities is challenging for many women, especially during a career transition. New job search activities, skill development, and family obligations can be demanding. You may face different expectations and pressures related to caregiving or household responsibilities, making it harder to allocate time and energy to your career transition. Women may need more representation in specific industries or leadership positions, and it can make it harder to envision yourself in new career paths. The absence of relatable role models and mentors may impact your confidence and motivation during the transition.

Women who have taken a career break for reasons such as caregiving, family responsibilities, or a traumatic event may face additional challenges when reentering the workforce. You may need more confidence in your employment history, updated skills, or a lack of confidence. Securing employment after a career break often requires addressing these challenges and highlighting transferable skills and experiences. Women may encounter systemic barriers in specific industries or organizations, such as limited opportunities for advancement, unequal access to leadership roles, or workplace cultures that perpetuate gender inequality. These systemic challenges can complicate a career transition and require women to navigate and challenge existing structures and biases.

Networking is crucial for career transitions, but women may need help accessing professional networks and opportunities. Male-dominated industries or social dynamics can limit your access to influential networks, making it more challenging to establish connections, find mentors, and gain visibility in their new field. Negotiating compensation and benefits is an important aspect of a career transition. However, research suggests that women often face obstacles in salary negotiations, leading to lower pay than their male counterparts. Overcoming this gender pay gap requires awareness, assertiveness, and practical negotiation skills.

Women may experience imposter syndrome—self-doubt and inadequacy despite their qualifications and accomplishments. During a career transition, imposter syndrome can be particularly challenging when entering unfamiliar territory. Building confidence and recognizing one's value and capabilities are crucial for overcoming this hurdle. Unfortunately, we live in a time when a woman's race can make a difference in career transition due to systemic biases and discrimination that can affect opportunities and experiences. It is essential to acknowledge that women from different racial and ethnic backgrounds may face unique challenges and barriers during their career transitions. Racial biases and discrimination can impact career opportunities and progression. Women from marginalized racial and ethnic backgrounds may face challenges such as racial stereotypes, limited access to networks, and unequal hiring, promotion, and pay treatment. These biases can affect their ability to transition to new careers or navigate upward mobility successfully. Women of different races and ethnicities may have varying access to resources that support career transition, such as mentorship, professional networks, and educational opportunities. Socioeconomic disparities and historical disadvantages can limit the availability of resources needed for successful career transitions. Cultural expectations and norms within different racial and ethnic communities can influence career choices and transitions. Factors such as family obligations, cultural expectations around specific professions, and limited exposure to particular industries or fields can impact career decision-making and mobility. I remember working with a professor who taught a finance course and had cultural issues with female students entering the field, subsequently making the course a living hell for them.

Addressing these systemic issues and creating inclusive and equitable environments that support women of all races and ethnicities in career transitions is essential. Organizations and individuals can take steps to challenge biases, promote diversity and inclusion, provide mentorship and support networks, and advocate for equal opportunities for women from all racial backgrounds. Additionally, women from marginalized racial and ethnic backgrounds have valuable perspectives and strengths that can contribute to diverse and inclusive workplaces. By recognizing and valuing these contributions, organizations can create environments where all women can thrive in career transitions.

One of my former professors who subsequently served on my dissertation committee, Dr. Nan Zhang Hampton, shared a story about facing a career transition due to a catastrophic event in her life. She lived in China, her home, and was in the first year of her residency as a new physician, and instantly, her life changed. A devastating earthquake crushed her legs, and she could no longer be a medical doctor. Instead of letting life defeat her, she pursued a Ph.D. and became a leading scholar and professor in rehabilitation studies. Before becoming one of the most successful authors of all time with the Harry Potter series, J.K. Rowling experienced significant transitions in her career. She worked as a researcher and bilingual secretary, but after the loss of her mother and a divorce, Rowling found herself on welfare and began writing the first Harry Potter book. The series' immense success led to her transition into a full-time career as a writer.

It's essential to recognize your challenges but also remember that you have unique strengths, perspectives, and abilities that can contribute to your success during a career transition. Building a solid support network, seeking mentors, and advocating for oneself can help you navigate these challenges and achieve your career goals. Vera Wang began her career as a figure skater and then transitioned into the fashion industry. She was an editor at Vogue magazine for many years before becoming a renowned fashion designer. Wang is mainly celebrated for her bridal and evening wear collections, dressing numerous celebrities and earning worldwide recognition in the fashion industry. Career transitions can lead to remarkable success if you allow yourself the grace to try. By following your passion, recognizing or creating new opportunities, and having the courage to pursue new paths, you can ultimately achieve incredible satisfaction. Building confidence and resilience is crucial during career transitions.

While preparing for my doctoral research, I stumbled upon a profound theory called transition theory. Transition theory was developed decades ago by a woman named Nancy Schlossberg. She developed this theory based on her experience transitioning to a new job in another state which she assumed would've been easy, yet it came with unexplained confusion and stress. Schlossberg developed three aspects to transition: anticipated, unanticipated, and nonevent. An anticipated transition is a significant life event that we expect to happen, such as starting a new job, changing careers, or starting a family. Unanticipated transitions are disruptive events such as a bad accident, severe illness, or a surprise promotion. A nonevent is an expected event that failed, such as not graduating, not getting a job you applied for, or not getting a promotion. The three transition events are significant because preparing for change is as salient as the change itself. Without self-awareness, your ability to adapt could be very good or bad.

As you transition through life, every year will bring new developments, some good and maybe some bad. Always remember that you are on a journey, and the destination, no matter how well you prepare, is not guaranteed. Start physically and emotionally preparing for transition; it will be a game changer. When you are contemplating transition, there are ten crucial steps to consider. They begin with you. Recognize your capabilities and celebrate your past achievements. Adopt a growth mindset and view challenges as learning opportunities. Remember that setbacks are a natural part of the process, and maintaining resilience will help you bounce back and stay focused on your goals.

Four

Career Preparation

"smart people learn from their own mistakes, and wise people learn from the mistakes of others" — *Unknown*

Preparation begins with you and your character, attitude, and abilities. Deciding on a career or business venture is essential to transitioning from a role to your purpose as you plan your journey to a new aspiration. When it comes time to make a choice think about every aspect of your life that will need changing; as you prepare for change, it is important to understand that change is not always easy, yet it can be one of the most rewarding things you'll ever do for yourself.

Ten Steps

Facing fears: Fear of failure is a common obstacle many people face. The fear of not succeeding or making mistakes can paralyze and prevent you from pursuing your aspirations.

Self-awareness: There is a reason why this is listed as number one. Take the time to evaluate and understand what motivates you and what you want to achieve in your career aspirations. Reflect on your strengths and weaknesses and any transferable skills you may have. One excellent evaluation is to conduct a SOAR analysis. What brings profound meaning to your life? Using inherent skills, your dreams, positions, and influence, you can create positive change and subsequently impact the lives of others.

Skills development: Identify gaps in your skill set and take steps to acquire the necessary skills. The necessary skills may involve additional education, certifications, or training programs. Look for opportunities to gain practical experience or volunteer in your desired field to enhance your expertise.

Your Network: Build a solid professional network in the area that you aspire to achieve. Attend events, join relevant online communities, and connect with professionals working in the field. Networking can provide valuable insights, mentorship, job leads, and potential references.

Your Credentials: Tailor your resume and cover letter to highlight the relevant skills and experiences you've acquired during your career transition. Emphasize transferable skills and showcase how your previous experience aligns with the new field. In addition, all of your experiences are a part of your credentials; speak about them in ways that align with your journey and aspirations.

Research: Develop an effective job search plan for your new career if this is your direction. Utilize online job boards, industry-specific websites, professional associations, and personal connections to identify potential job opportunities. Consider informational interviews and job shadowing to understand specific roles better.

Flexibility and adaptability: Be open to starting at a lower level or taking on new responsibilities initially. Recognize that a career transition may involve starting from scratch or taking a different path than your previous role. Be prepared for a learning curve and embrace growth opportunities.

Persistence and perseverance: Career transitions can be challenging, and setbacks are common. Stay focused, remain motivated, and don't get discouraged. Keep refining your approach, seeking feedback, and adapting your strategies.

Continuous learning: Commit to lifelong learning and professional development. Stay updated on trends, technologies, and best practices in your desired field. Seek out training programs, workshops, webinars, blogs, and other educational resources to stay ahead in your career.

Your support: Don't hesitate to seek support from mentors, career coaches, or support groups during your career transition. They can provide guidance, advice, and emotional support as you navigate the challenges and uncertainties of changing careers. Remember, career preparation requires time, effort, and perseverance. With the right mindset, planning, and proactive approach, you can successfully navigate your way into a rewarding new career. Throughout your career, you will face many situations that will challenge various aspects of your development, particularly – grit and outcome. These components are vitally important; having one without the other can play a vital role in your career decision-making. People with grit achieve results that transcend everyday organizational imperatives and outcomes. Employers today want you to know and practice communication, teamwork, and critical thinking (problem-solving). It would be best to prepare yourself first to lead before you can lead others successfully. Here are essential attributes as you prepare for a career change, planning, or direction.

Build Empathetic Relationships

- Demonstrate empathy one-on-one, both personally and professionally.

- Show genuine appreciation to family, friends, and colleagues as individuals.

- Build trust, do what you say, and say what you mean.

Demonstrate Excitement

- If you show excitement in what you do, you will ignite excitement in others.

- People will see and understand what drives you.

- Passion reminds you and shows others why you are doing what you do.

Emotional Intelligence

- Demonstrate the skill to control your emotional state.

- Show the ability to actively and effectively listen as if you were in others' shoes.

- Show appreciation for people's efforts no matter how difficult the situation or conversation.

Paying Yourself First

- We all get up every day and serve others in some capacity. But the reality is that if we do not care about ourselves, our reputations, and our personal brands, it is a given that nobody else will. So you must resolve to pay yourself first and give yourself the time and attention you need to create and develop your brand. This practice will pay you back tenfold over time.

Performance Accountability

- Accept responsibility for the outcomes expected of you.
- Establish a structure for accomplishing goals, particularly SMART goals.
- Use a SOAR Analysis to understand your strengths, opportunities, aspirations, and results.
- Ask yourself how to improve the situation, make a difference, and do it.

Take on Leadership Roles

- Making time to take on leadership roles is vital to your brand and your career. As you think of your leadership goals and what roles might help you accomplish them: don't join ten groups; join two. And make sure you can be a leader in one of them.

Active Listening

- Respond to what is being said rather than what you want to hear. Refrain from answering someone's question midway through their sentence. Just listen.
- Allow people to tell their whole story. Ask them for permission to recall or summarize what you heard to demonstrate that you were engaged.

Make Yourself the Focal Point

- As you develop your brand, one of the most important things you need to consider is your network. This lets you spread the word about who you are and what you can do.

Dealing with Conflict

- Consider additional ways that the situation could have been handled. Sometimes we don't consider positive intent, and as a result, we misunderstand someone's intention.

- Always focus on the problem, not the person. This process brings everything back to reality.

- Ask colleagues what they would do if they were in your shoes. This can help you look at things with a different view.

- Ask yourself how everything would be if it were going well (in a perfect world)

Convey Your Authority

- We often fail to get recognition because our credibility is undefined, or people need to be more specific. Think through ways to convey your authority so that people understand the expertise you are bringing to the table. Develop your credibility.

Career Growth

- Ask yourself what your career would look like if you couldn't fail. At times we need to remember to dream. This question will allow you to think outside of your current state.

- Remember the creative things you are good at without getting paid for them. This thinking can open up thoughts that were never considered before.

- Ask yourself what your ideal career would look like. Asking will make you consider the choices that you've made or are considering.

- Think about what motivates you to achieve your goals (personal or professional.) Motivation creates action; action creates opportunities.

Move Where the Trend is Going

- Put yourself where the trend is going. Find a niche with growth, learn everything you can about it, write about it, and get the momentum to build your name and reputation as an authority on that topic. This allows you to move where the trend is going.

Be Willing to Abandon Your Strengths

- One key to success is being bold and persistent in what has worked well. What will help you get to where you want to be?

Are there strengths you need to walk away from and other areas to focus on and learn more about? If so, start formulating a plan to make that happen.

Here are a few stories of everyday people that have changed careers based on following the things they have always loved. These stories highlight individuals who intentionally pursue career paths aligned with their passions and values. While their journeys may not be as widely known as those of famous figures, they showcase the courage, determination, and fulfillment that can come from making a career change in pursuit of personal happiness and purpose.

Sarah had a successful career as a marketing manager, but she always had a deep love for animals. She decided to transition into animal welfare and started volunteering at a local animal shelter in her spare time. Inspired by the experience, she pursued other animal behavior and welfare education. Eventually, Sarah landed a job as an animal welfare advocate, dedicating her career to improving the lives of animals and raising awareness about their rights. Emily worked as an accountant for several years but always had a passion for photography. She decided to take a leap of faith and pursue a career change. Sarah enrolled in photography courses built a portfolio, and started taking on freelance projects. Over time, she gained recognition for her talent and now runs a successful photography business, capturing special moments for clients. After working in the corporate world for several years, Jane realized her true passion was for yoga and wellness. Despite the uncertainty and financial challenges, she pursued yoga teacher training and started teaching classes. Over time, she built a successful career as a yoga instructor and found fulfillment in helping others achieve physical and mental well-being. Sarah worked as a lawyer in a corporate firm, but her deep concern for the environment led her to seek a career change. She joined a nonprofit organization focused on environmental advocacy and conservation. Sarah's transition allowed her to align her professional life with her values and contribute to meaningful environmental causes.

Career preparation sets you up for success by providing clarity, goal-setting skill development, strategies, networking opportunities, and adaptability. It helps you navigate career paths, make informed decisions, and effectively compete in the job market, leading to fulfilling and rewarding professional lives.

Five

Career Preparation for Entrepreneurs

Career success for entrepreneurs is defined by achieving business goals, personal fulfillment, and financial growth; however, success looks different to every entrepreneur. Some entrepreneurs do not even call themselves entrepreneurs; they say, business owners. Many ma & pa owners run their business just like going to any day job. Some enjoy it immensely and create new ways to diversify their products and services. And others provide the same thing, looking the same way and getting the same results. Successful entrepreneurs have a clear vision and set specific, measurable goals to guide their actions. They define their purpose, identify their target market, and establish a roadmap to success.

Suppose you dream of becoming an entrepreneur or stumble into the beautiful world of business ownership. In that case, several key factors contribute to entrepreneurial career success, beginning with passion and persistence. Many entrepreneurs think their age makes a difference, but your passion and persistence make the difference. Arianna Huffington, known for co-founding The Huffington Post, started the online news and blog platform in her late forties. She was crucial in building it into a prominent media outlet before selling it to AOL. Masaru Ibuka co-founded Sony Corporation at the age of 54. Along with his business partner Akio Morita, Ibuka built Sony into a prominent electronics company known for its innovative products and technologies. These examples demonstrate that age should not be a limiting factor in entrepreneurship. These entrepreneurs found success later in life by leveraging their unique experiences, skills, and passions. Their stories inspire others to pursue their entrepreneurial aspirations, regardless of age, and highlight the potential for achieving remarkable success in business at any stage of life. Passion fuels motivation and drives entrepreneurs to overcome challenges and persevere despite obstacles. Building a successful career as an entrepreneur requires a strong belief in the value of their product or service and the determination to push through setbacks and failures.

Running a business is often marked by uncertainty and challenges. It takes resilience, willingness to pivot your strategies, learn from failures, and bounce back from setbacks. You must view challenges as opportunities for growth and use them as stepping stones to further success. Sara Blakely, the founder of Spanx, a shapewear company, faced multiple rejections from manufacturers and potential investors before launching her product. Blakely overcame skepticism and persevered, eventually building Spanx into a highly successful and globally recognized brand. Sophia Amoruso encountered various challenges and setbacks on her path to success. She founded Nasty Gal, an online fashion retailer, but faced financial and legal issues. Despite these obstacles, Amoruso demonstrated resilience and adapted her business model, ultimately achieving success with her brand and empowering women entrepreneurs through her work. These entrepreneurs showcase the strength, determination, and resilience to overcome uncertainty and challenges. Their stories inspire, highlighting that success can be achieved despite setbacks, and remind them of the importance of perseverance and resilience on the entrepreneurial journey.

As stated, successful entrepreneurs recognize the importance of continuous learning and self-improvement to be influential leaders. They stay updated on industry trends, emerging technologies, and market shifts. They seek out mentors, attend workshops, read relevant books, and actively pursue knowledge that enhances their business acumen. Entrepreneurs who build successful careers understand the importance of effective leadership and team building. They assemble a skilled and motivated team, delegate responsibilities, and foster a positive and collaborative work culture. They inspire and empower employees to perform at their best and contribute to the business's success.

As you embark on your business journey, you must have a solid understanding of financial management. This may be one of the first things you should discuss with a mentor or colleague with similar interests. Seek professional advice to help manage your resources wisely. Keeping your eye on cash flow, maintaining accurate financial records, and making informed decisions based on financial data is critical.

Entrepreneurs who prioritize their customer's needs and build strong relationships tend to experience long-term success. They listen to customer feedback, constantly seek ways to improve their products or services, and prioritize exceptional customer experiences. Building trust and loyalty with customers can lead to repeat business, referrals, and positive word-of-mouth. Career success for entrepreneurs includes finding a balance between work and personal life. Successful entrepreneurs prioritize their well-being, maintain healthy boundaries, and ensure they have time for family, hobbies, and self-care. They recognize that long-term success requires sustainable practices and self-care to avoid burnout. It's important to note that entrepreneurial success is unique to each individual, and the path to success may vary. However, incorporating these key factors into your career increases your chances of achieving your business goals and finding fulfillment in your entrepreneurial journey. Another critical aspect of the preparation is research.

The U.S. Bureau of Labor Statistics (https://www.bls.gov/audience/jobseekers.htm) provides a variety of valuable reports on employment statistics and 10-year forecasts. Check it out to establish if your chosen career is experiencing, or is likely to experience, a talent shortage. If so, you can expect a higher starting salary or more appealing perks if your skills match employers' needs. Test your work-related skill set at Mind Tools (https://www.mindtools.com) to discover how your competencies, such as communication, critical thinking, and stress management, add up. Then use the self-development career resources they provide to build your skills and become more attractive to prospective employers.

Career research is a continuing process. Consistently gather information, refine your understanding of potential career paths, and adapt your goals accordingly. Staying updated on industry news, trends, and emerging technologies through online publications, blogs, podcasts, and industry-specific forums is critical for getting a better understanding of not only the industry but the overall culture of that industry. Engage in discussions, join relevant online communities, and follow thought leaders in your field of interest. Check out resources on Linkedin, Meetup, and even Tik Tok have opportunities to learn and meet like-minded people. This ongoing research helps you stay informed about evolving opportunities and skill requirements. Join professional associations related to your areas of interest. Attend industry conferences, seminars, and networking events. These platforms provide opportunities to connect with professionals, gain industry-specific insights, and learn about potential career paths. Many associations also offer career resources, mentorship programs, and job boards. Combining self-assessment, exploring diverse resources, and engaging with professionals allows you to make well-informed decisions and discover exciting career opportunities.

Six

Self-Awareness

> *"Knowing others is intelligence, knowing yourself is true wisdom, Mastering others is strength, Mastering yourself is true power"* — *Lao-Tsu*

Becoming self-aware is a journey, not a destination, and it is free. It takes patience, constant evaluation, and reflection. You must fully grasp your emotional well-being to deal with stress and overall life changes created by the onset of maturity. Emotional well-being can be defined as one's ability to: feel comfortable with self, relate to others, handle disappointment, solve problems, celebrate successes, and think critically (Page & Page, 1992). We generally do not anticipate the emotional stress and the changes we will experience in developing ourselves for career transition or transformation. Let us dissect the definition of self-awareness. If awareness is the ability to know, feel or perceive, then self-awareness is knowing, feeling, or perceiving things about yourself. As a society, the usual way in which we gain an understanding of ourselves is through experiences and our reactions to those experiences. Although trial and error play a natural part in human evolution, you should be more purposeful in advancing your self-awareness. As mentioned, utilize a SOAR analysis to evaluate your strengths, opportunities, aspirations, and results. Take time to reflect on the results instead of judging them; you might find that who you *think* you are conflicts with who you are. There is an excellent book, a classic called *Do What You Are*, that I highly recommend. This book is my favorite of all career preparation books because the authors emphasize concentrating on who you are, and the rest will fall into place. According to the authors, when you are in the most fulfilling job, you should:

- Look forward to going to work
- Feel energized (most of the time) by what you do
- Feel your contribution is respected and appreciated

- Feel proud when describing your work to others
- Enjoy and respect the people you work with
- Feel optimistic about your future

Knowing who you are is the most critical and vital aspect of career satisfaction. You might not know your life's purpose at this point in your journey. Your life will constantly evolve, changing more times than you can count. However, as you prepare for your career journey, being aware of yourself and what is meaningful to you is critical. There will come a time when you realize that your attitude and behavior are fundamental to how you are perceived and embraced or how you perceive and embrace others. When people trust you, you never have to wonder; when they follow you, always do the right thing. The behaviors below are essential to achieving personal growth and a positive mindset.

Optimism: Be hopeful, encouraged, and believe situations can be resolved due to your actions.

Inspiration: Find inspirational and motivational quotes. Memorize and say them every day.

Empathy: Treat your feelings and the feelings of others with dignity and understanding.

Listening: Give others your full attention without judgment.

Celebrate: Do not take your achievements for granted. Enjoy, honor, and praise your achievements, even if no one else seems to notice.

Love: Love what you do and who you are, and give love without the expectations of receiving it back.

Giving: Give back to your peers, community, and others in need.

I had a profound "aha" moment as I was reading *Leadership in the Crucible of Work* for one of my doctorate classes, and the author mentioned that the word "passion" is vastly misunderstood. He stated that most people believe that passion is something you feel strongly about or want badly; however, he said we need to be corrected. He stated that passion is defined by what you are willing to sacrifice. Defining passion as what you're willing to sacrifice was most profound because I have always used passion as one of my values. Knowing that the root of the word passion comes from the Latin word *passire*, meaning to suffer, as in the unfathomable sacrifice of suffering in the Passion of Christ, brought a whole new meaning. At that point, I understood the connection; knowing your passion in life gives you a sense of purpose. It's what you're willing to sacrifice having less of, including sleep, love, food, travel, or money. Take the time to find yours because where, how, and what you find may surprise you.

One day I took the time to reflect on what was most important to me in my life and career. I had a great job, loved my work, however, I did not feel a connection to the industry I was working in. I had no desire to pursue moving up the ladder. So I decided to leave corporate America to pursue a career in academia, a lifelong aspiration. I paid attention to my fears, apprehension, and capabilities. I packed up and moved to a new city, started a Life & Career Coaching course, and started making calls for teaching opportunities in higher education. I also told everyone in my professional circle that I was transitioning and pursuing teaching. Within three months, I landed a job as an adjunct professor at San Diego State University. I focused on my strengths rather than on what I could have done better. I pursued a doctorate to stay on course in my new career. I sacrificed seeing my family and friends, attending events, and traveling to finish my degree because I was passionate about why I was doing it. When I reflect, all of my sacrifices have been fruitful and made me who I have become and do what I love. My friend Dr. Eric Thomas stated that you would persist when you want what you are doing more than you want to breathe. As you are reflecting on your passion, think of what it is in life that you cannot do without. Your passion for something may be a hobby, i.e., you must work out, write poetry, create new music or some other art form, travel, etc. Bill Gates and Steve Jobs sacrificed finishing college to pursue their passion. I encourage you to find something in life that you need or believe in so severely that you'll make sacrifices for it. Knowledge is defined as awareness or familiarity gained by experience of a fact or situation. Knowledge is your key to greatness. The ways of the world are at your fingertips. The more you are self-aware about what you want to pursue as a career, the more power you give yourself to make the best decisions. Yes, knowledge is power. Knowledge is impressionable, influential, and a game changer.

When looking at career knowledge, think about the industry, companies, and jobs within that trade and ask yourself, will I enjoy these duties, tasks, and responsibilities? Will I be proud of the work I do daily? Do I get to be creative, or is it more routine? Is it challenging and rewarding? Does the work fit into my long-term career objectives?

Will it offer a variety of work assignments? How much autonomy will I have? Is the nature of the work more project-oriented? Will I be working with people, ideas, data, or things? Can I balance the duties with my other commitments? Does the work involve intangibles or concrete and observable outcomes? Does it require leadership skills, or can I be more of an independent contributor? What's the workload? The most important thing to remember is that you are what you do, so finding something purposeful is critical to personal satisfaction.

It would help if you strived to have a deep and personal connection to your daily work. You bring your best to work every day when you have a personal connection. Your happiness, confidence, and influence will increase during good or bad times. You will care about the people you work with in a meaningful manner. Your alignment should begin with knowing your top five values. When I was teaching, I gave values exercises in my leadership classes. One day a student told me frustratingly that he spent three hours trying to narrow down his top five values. My question to him was, when did you last spend three hours devoted to knowing yourself? He said never! Many of my students thought this lesson was necessary when they were interviewed. I learned this lesson the hard way.

Years ago, when I worked in the music industry, I was interviewed for an important position at a major record label. I was very prepared for and confident about the interview. Upon meeting with the VP, she told me my recommendations were solid, my resume was excellent, and I probably knew a lot about the company. As a result, she began the interview by asking me to tell her a little about myself. No problem! Next, she asked what are your top five values? I remember, as if yesterday, the sinking feeling I had as I was trying hard to come up with a truthful answer, which was written all over my face. I thought to myself, be honest, so I smiled and said, "I have never thought about this, and would you mind if I called you tomorrow with the answer after I put intentional thought to it?." She said yes and resumed the interview.

Although the rest of the interview went well, I could not get past not knowing my values. I felt stupid for not knowing the answer - it was about me! I called her the following day and gave my values. She thanked me and said that knowing my values was vital because they are a significant aspect of what I would bring to work daily. She spoke of the importance of my values aligning with the organization's values.

It was one of the most important lessons I learned about myself. I share it constantly so that others will not be unprepared.

It would be best if you had a personal connection to who you are and what in life is most meaningful to you today. Your values will change over time as your priorities in life will change, but wherever you are in your journey, be intentional about your values. Your values must align with your purpose, passion, knowledge, and personality. Knowing thyself is the most important aspect of a healthy, happy, and fulfilling career. Many people are great at interviews and can say all the right things about their knowledge of the position. It's when employers begin digging deeper into our knowledge about who we are personally is when the disconnect becomes apparent. Being authentic is easy when you are true to yourself. Being self-aware is a critical step to knowing what you stand for.

Seven

Skills & Ability Development

Identifying gaps in your skill set and taking steps to acquire the necessary skills is paramount. This may involve pursuing additional education, certifications, or training programs. Reflect on your current skills and abilities and identify areas where you want to improve or acquire new competencies. Consider the skills relevant to your career goals or areas that align with your interests and personal development. Once you have an idea of the career direction you would like to explore, begin setting specific skills development goals. Break down your goals into smaller, manageable tasks you can work on incrementally. Establish a timeline and milestones to track your progress. As I have mentioned previously, create SMART goals so that you are intentional.

When I realized I wanted to excel in higher education, I returned to school for a doctorate. The fantastic thing is that even after leaving higher education, having a doctorate has opened many doors. Embrace a mindset of continuous learning. Go after opportunities for formal education, such as courses, workshops, or certifications, either online or in-person. Leverage online learning platforms, educational institutions, or professional development programs offered by employers or industry associations. Also, engage with experts and experienced professionals in your field of interest whenever you can. Seek their guidance, ask for advice, and learn from their experiences. Mentorship programs, networking events, and industry conferences provide opportunities to connect with people who can impart valuable knowledge. Actively seek feedback from mentors, supervisors, or peers to gauge your progress and identify areas for improvement. Constructive feedback helps you understand your strengths and weaknesses, allowing you to focus your development efforts more effectively. Skills develop through consistent practice and real-world application. Look for opportunities to apply your skills in practical settings, such as internships, volunteering, or freelance work. Apply your knowledge and seek feedback to refine and improve your abilities.

To confront fears and trepidation, you should step out of your comfort zone and take on challenges that push your boundaries. Embracing challenges allows you to develop resilience, problem-solving skills, and adaptability. Engage in projects or activities that require you to stretch your abilities and learn new skills. Regularly reflect on your progress and growth. Assess how your skills and abilities have evolved. Identify areas where you have made significant improvements and areas that still need development. Self-reflection helps you stay focused, motivated, and aware of your personal and professional growth.

Take advantage of online resources, such as tutorials, webinars, blogs, and video courses, which provide a wealth of knowledge across various domains. Online platforms like LinkedIn Learning, Coursera, Udemy, and Khan Academy offer various courses and tutorials to develop specific skills. Remember, skills and abilities development is a lifelong journey. Continuously assess, learn, practice, and seek growth opportunities. Developing a diverse skill set enhances your employability and equips you with the tools to adapt to changing work environments and pursue new opportunities throughout your career. Credentials, such as degrees, certifications, or licenses, provide tangible evidence of your knowledge and expertise in a specific field. They validate your skills and competence, giving employers and industry professionals confidence in your abilities during a career transition. Having relevant credentials can set you apart from other candidates and increase your chances of securing new opportunities.

A resume and cover letter highlighting your relevant skills and experiences is always necessary; however, emphasizing transferable skills and showcasing your previous experience and how they align with your new journey is key. All of your experiences are a part of your credentials; speak about them in ways that align with your journey and aspirations. Many organizations are beginning not to require a bachelor's degree and are focusing more on relevant experience and ability. Specific industries or professions have established standards and requirements that candidates must meet. Credentials demonstrate that you have met these standards, positioning you as a qualified candidate in your career transition. They showcase your commitment to professional growth and adherence to industry best practices.

Skills and ability development are crucial for personal and professional growth. Here are some reputable and popular skills assessments available for individuals changing careers:

- Myers-Briggs Type Indicator (MBTI): The MBTI assesses personality preferences and can help individuals understand their natural strengths, communication style, and work preferences. It provides insights into how your personality aligns with different career paths.

- StrengthsFinder: StrengthsFinder focuses on identifying your innate talents and strengths. It helps you uncover your top strengths and suggests how you can leverage them in your career. This assessment can clarify what you excel at and guide your career choices.

- DISC Assessment: The DISC assessment measures your behavioral style and communication preferences. It categorizes individuals into four main personality types (Dominance, Influence, Steadiness, and Conscientiousness) and can help you understand how your style fits into different work environments.

- SkillsFuture Skills Assessment: SkillsFuture is a Singapore government initiative offering various skills assessments and profiling tools. It helps individuals identify their current skill sets and gaps and recommends suitable training and development programs.

- *O*NET Interest Profiler: The *O*NET Interest Profiler is an online assessment that helps you identify your interests and how they relate to various occupations. It provides a list of careers that align with your interests, helping you explore new career paths.

- CliftonStrengths Assessment: The CliftonStrengths assessment (formerly known as StrengthsFinder) focuses on identifying your unique strengths and provides insights into leveraging them in your career. It helps you understand how your strengths can contribute to different roles and industries.

- CareerLeader: CareerLeader is a comprehensive career assessment tool that evaluates your interests, motivators, and skills. It provides personalized feedback on potential career paths that align with your profile and offer insights into the skills and competencies needed for those careers.

It's important to note that while these assessments can provide valuable insights, they should be used as a starting point and not as definitive measures of your abilities or career choices. Consider working with a career coach or counselor who can help interpret the results and guide you through the career exploration process. should be used Be honest when utilizing career assessment tools to assist you in evaluating your strengths and weakness because what you put in is what you get out.

Eight
Your Network

It is important to note that building and maintaining a solid network requires cultivating genuine relationships, being responsive and supportive, and offering value to others. Many people recognize the power of their networks and strategically leverage their connections to enhance their careers, expand their influence, and access new opportunities. Often people collaborate with others in their industry or the industry that they plan to expand their reach and create mutually beneficial opportunities. These collaborations can involve joint projects, endorsements, or partnerships that allow you to tap into each other's networks, expertise, and resources. Approach networking with a genuine interest in building relationships rather than solely focusing on what others can offer you. Seek ways to provide value, whether sharing industry insights, offering assistance, or making introductions. Building authentic relationships based on mutual respect and support can lead to long-term connections beneficial for your career change.

Jay-Z, the renowned rapper, and entrepreneur, utilized his network to enhance his career in multiple ways. He formed strategic alliances with fellow musicians, producers, and industry insiders. These connections helped him secure record deals, collaborate on successful albums, and launch his ventures. Jay-Z's network extended beyond music, as he leveraged relationships with business leaders and celebrities to expand his influence in fashion, sports management, and entrepreneurship. Being part of a network provides access to resources, expertise, and support. You can tap into their network's knowledge, connections, and resources for various needs, such as professional advice, access to specialized services, or opportunities to showcase their work to a broader audience. You will often receive referrals and recommendations from their network connections. These referrals can lead to new jobs, roles, collaborations, or endorsements. Recommendations from influential individuals within their network carry weight and can open doors to high-profile opportunities.

Kim Kardashian West, the reality television star and businesswoman, has utilized her network to build a media empire. She has cultivated relationships with influential figures in the fashion, beauty, and entertainment industries, allowing her to launch successful brands and collaborations. Kardashian West's network has provided her with platforms for endorsements, partnerships, and opportunities to expand her business ventures. Rihanna, the singer, actress, and entrepreneur, has harnessed the power of her network to enhance her career in various ways. She cultivated relationships with industry professionals, including record executives, producers, and designers. These connections helped her secure record deals, collaborate on hit songs, and launch successful fashion and beauty brands. Rihanna's network has played a pivotal role in her rise to global stardom and influence in multiple industries. These examples demonstrate how famous people strategically utilize their networks to enhance their careers. These individuals have achieved remarkable success in their respective fields by cultivating valuable relationships, tapping into expertise, and accessing resources and opportunities.

Another important way to network is through volunteer work or joining professional groups related to your desired career. Volunteering can help you meet like-minded individuals, develop new skills, and gain exposure to different aspects of the industry. Many times people have found their calling or purpose through volunteering. Additionally, professional groups often host networking events and offer opportunities for collaboration and learning. Remember, building a network takes time and effort. Be proactive, consistent, and genuine in your interactions. Cultivate relationships by maintaining regular contact, expressing gratitude, and offering assistance when possible. A strong network can provide valuable guidance, support, and opportunities as you navigate your career change.

As you conduct research, consider career commonality, which refers to shared experiences, challenges, or characteristics among individuals in specific career paths or industries. It recognizes that people pursuing similar careers may encounter similar circumstances, opportunities, and hurdles along their professional journeys. Career commonality can manifest in various ways.

Occupational Challenges: Certain careers have inherent challenges or shared experiences that professionals in those fields can relate to. For example, doctors may face long hours, high-stress levels, and ethical dilemmas, creating a commonality among healthcare professionals.

Industry Trends and Dynamics: Industries often have unique trends, practices, and dynamics that shape the experiences of professionals within them. This can create commonalities regarding skill requirements, job demands, and professional development opportunities. For instance, individuals in the technology sector may share a common experience of rapid innovation and the need for continuous learning.

Professional Networks and Communities: Professionals in the same career field often form networks and communities to share insights, support, and resources. These networks foster a sense of commonality and provide a platform for professionals to connect, exchange knowledge, and navigate shared challenges.

Career Transitions and Development: Individuals going through similar career transitions, such as starting a business, changing industries, or pursuing further education, may find commonality in the challenges, uncertainties, and opportunities they encounter during these transformative periods.

Career commonality can provide support, camaraderie, and shared learning among professionals. It allows you to connect with others who understand your experiences and can provide guidance or empathy. Commonality can foster collaboration, mentorship, and the sharing of best practices, ultimately enhancing professional growth and success within a specific career path or industry.

It is important to note that while career commonality exists, each individual's career journey is still unique. Personal aspirations, backgrounds, and circumstances shape an individual's experience within a given career. Recognizing the commonalities and individuality within careers can help you build meaningful connections while embracing your unique path.

The Career Renaissance

Nine
Flexibility & Adaptability

Career transitions can be daunting, especially when moving into a new field. Flexibility and adaptability are essential qualities to cultivate during a career transition. Here's why they are important. Career transitions often involve significant changes, such as family obligations, switching industries, roles, or work environments. Flexibility and adaptability allow you to embrace these changes with an open mindset. Instead of resisting or fearing change, you can view it as an opportunity for growth and new experiences.

Career transitions often require acquiring new skills or updating existing ones. Flexibility allows you to be open to learning and developing these skills, even if they are outside your comfort zone. Being adaptable means quickly adjusting and adapting to the demands of the new career and acquiring the necessary knowledge and abilities to thrive. Lady Gaga started her career as a pop singer known for her eccentric and avant-garde style. However, she has constantly evolved and adapted her image and musical style. Gaga has showcased her versatility by exploring different genres, collaborating with diverse artists, and taking on acting roles. Her ability to adapt and push boundaries has contributed to her success and critical acclaim.

Pursuing a new career can come with uncertainties, including job prospects, income stability, or job security. Flexibility and adaptability help you navigate these uncertainties by remaining open to different possibilities and adjusting your plans. They enable you to explore alternative paths, consider different options, and adapt your approach to changing circumstances. Flexibility and adaptability enable you to recognize and seize potential opportunities during your career transition. Being open to new possibilities allows you to capitalize on unexpected job openings, networking connections, or emerging trends in your desired field. By adapting your plans and being flexible, you can position yourself to take advantage of these opportunities. A career change can be challenging, and setbacks may occur. Fostering resilience will allow you to bounce back from setbacks and persevere through obstacles. Will Smith began his career as a rapper and transitioned into acting, successfully adapting to different genres and mediums. He gained popularity with his hit TV show "The Fresh Prince of Bel-Air" and became a box office star with roles in action films, comedies, and dramas. Smith's ability to adapt his acting style and take on varied roles has solidified his status as a versatile and successful actor.

Flexibility and adaptability encourage a mindset of continuous learning and personal growth. They encourage embracing new ideas, technologies, and industry trends. Being adaptable allows you to quickly adjust to changes in your field and proactively seek opportunities to develop new skills or expand your knowledge. Flexibility and adaptability are valuable traits when building a professional network. They allow you to connect with people from diverse backgrounds, industries, and perspectives. By being adaptable in your interactions, you can establish meaningful connections, collaborate with others, and tap into new opportunities that may arise through networking. Actor Charlize Theron has demonstrated her flexibility and adaptability through her transformative performances. She has taken on diverse roles ranging from intense dramas like "Monster," for which she won an Academy Award, to action-packed films like "Mad Max: Fury Road." Theron's commitment to fully immersing herself in her characters and willingness to embrace challenging and diverse roles have contributed to her success and critical acclaim.

In summary, flexibility and adaptability are vital for a successful career transition. They allow you to embrace change, learn new skills, overcome challenges, seize opportunities, build connections, evolve with the job market, and maintain a growth mindset. By cultivating these qualities, you can navigate transitions more effectively and thrive in your new career path.

Ten

Habits

Habits are regular, often unconscious, routines or behaviors you develop over time through recurrence. They can be good and bad, impacting various aspects of your life, including your career. Habits shape your actions, thoughts, and responses and can significantly influence your productivity, success, and overall well-being. If you are unaware of how they impact your behavior, your habits can make or break your career plans. Recognize that a career change may involve stepping out of your comfort zone and adjusting to new environments, technologies, and work processes.

Habits are often performed automatically, without conscious thought. They are ingrained into our daily routines and become second nature. This automaticity makes habits powerful because they require less mental effort and decision-making. In the book *Atomic Habits*, the author shares a scenario asking you to imagine you have a messy room, and your goal is to clean it. If you take the time to make it tidy, you will have a clean room for the moment. However, if you have sloppy habits, it will take a little while before the room is messy again. You will find yourself facing the same outcome over and over again because you are dealing with the symptom and not the cause. Habits involve repetitive actions or behaviors. They are performed consistently over time, creating a habitual pattern or routine. Consistency is crucial for habits to form and have a lasting impact. Specific cues or contexts often trigger habits in general. Certain situations, environments, or emotional states can act as triggers for activating a habit. For example, stress at work may trigger the habit of reaching for unhealthy snacks. Let us examine a few habits that need to be avoided as you are preparing for your career transition.

Avoid procrastination, which can hinder your progress and delay your career change. Break tasks into smaller, manageable steps and create a schedule to keep yourself accountable and motivated. Be mindful of negative self-talk and self-doubt. Cultivate a habit of positive thinking and belief in your abilities. Surround yourself with supportive and encouraging people who uplift and inspire you. Refrain from the habit of resisting change. Instead, embrace the opportunities with a career transition and be open to new possibilities. Remember that change often leads to personal and professional growth. If you have a habit of neglecting to plan, it can impede your career change progress. Develop the habit of setting clear objectives, creating a strategy, and outlining action steps to achieve your goals. A well-thought-out plan will keep you focused and organized during the transition. Last but not least, avoid isolating yourself during a career change. Cultivate the habit of seeking support from mentors, friends, or career coaches who can provide guidance, advice, and encouragement. Connect with others who have undergone similar transitions to learn from their experiences.

By developing positive habits and avoiding detrimental habits, you can set yourself up for a successful career change and increase your chances of achieving your desired outcomes. Understanding the nature of habits allows us to harness their power in shaping our careers and professional lives. We can improve our productivity, work performance, and overall career satisfaction by consciously cultivating positive habits and breaking free from negative ones. Drew Barrymore struggled with substance abuse and personal challenges during her early years in Hollywood. Through determination and a strong desire for change, she sought help, embraced sobriety, and focused on building a healthier lifestyle. Barrymore established herself as a successful actress, producer, and businesswoman. Jennifer Lopez worked hard to break the habit of settling for less and being typecast in specific roles. She pursued her passion for acting and music, consistently pushing herself outside her comfort zone. By breaking free from limiting beliefs and embracing new challenges, Lopez became a successful actress, singer, and businesswoman. These celebrities demonstrate that breaking bad habits is possible and can lead to personal growth, transformation, and career success. They serve as inspiring examples of individuals who faced challenges, committed to change, and overcame obstacles to achieve greatness in their respective fields.

There can be societal and cultural factors that contribute to certain habits hindering women more than men. It is important to note that these habits may not be universal, and individual experiences may vary. Here are a few examples of habits that can disproportionately impact women. More often than men, women may apologize unnecessarily, even for things beyond their control or responsibility.

This habit can undermine confidence and assertiveness and may contribute to women being perceived as less authoritative in professional settings. Due to societal expectations and pressures, women may be more prone to overthinking, self-doubt, and seeking perfection. This can lead to indecisiveness and a fear of taking risks, potentially hindering career advancement and opportunities for growth. Women may habitually downplay their accomplishments and not fully embrace their successes. This habit can impact self-promotion and hinder their visibility in the workplace, potentially affecting career progression and recognition. Women, often due to societal expectations and caregiving roles, may have a habit of overextending themselves and prioritizing the needs of others over their own. These actions can lead to burnout and a lack of focus on personal and professional growth. Women may be less inclined to negotiate for higher salaries, promotions, or better work conditions than their male counterparts. This habit can contribute to gender pay gaps and disparities in career advancement.

It is essential to recognize that various social, cultural, and organizational factors influence these habits. Addressing these habits requires collective efforts to challenge gender stereotypes, promote equal opportunities, and create inclusive work environments where both women and men can thrive. Encouraging self-empowerment, assertiveness training, and mentorship programs can help women overcome these habits and achieve career success. If you are having issues with changing your habits, the problem may be someone other than you but your system.

Systems thinking is a practical approach that can significantly assist in career development. It will help you understand and navigate the complexities of the career landscape by considering the interconnectedness (how does A affect B, C, D, etc.) of various elements and the broader context in which your career operates. In other words, a systems thinking mindset helps you look at the big picture: how finances affect family, how time at work affects personal growth, how health affects productivity, etc. Here are some ways that systems thinking can be beneficial.

Holistic Perspective: Systems thinking encourages a holistic view of career development. Instead of focusing solely on individual actions or isolated career decisions, it considers personal strengths, skills, values, family, industry trends, market demands, and societal influences. This broader perspective helps you make more informed and well-rounded career choices.

Identifying Patterns and Relationships: Systems thinking allows you to identify patterns, feedback loops, and relationships between different elements within the career system. It helps uncover the underlying dynamics and influences that impact career development. Understanding these relationships allows you to make strategic decisions and leverage opportunities more effectively.

Navigating and Anticipating Change: Career landscapes are dynamic and subject to change. Systems thinking equips you with the ability to anticipate and navigate these changes. It helps you recognize emerging trends, disruptions, and shifts in industries or job markets. Again, by understanding the interconnectedness of various elements, you can proactively adapt their skills, knowledge, and strategies to stay relevant and seize new opportunities.

Leveraging Interdisciplinary Skills: Systems thinking draws upon interdisciplinary skills and knowledge. It encourages you to integrate insights from psychology, sociology, economics, and technology into your career development process. This interdisciplinary approach enables you to analyze career challenges from multiple perspectives and uncover innovative solutions.

Long-Term Career Planning: Systems thinking emphasizes long-term career planning rather than focusing solely on short-term goals. It encourages you to consider the broader trajectory of their careers and anticipate the potential consequences of their decisions. By taking a systems view, you can set meaningful and sustainable career goals that align with your values, strengths, and long-term aspirations.

Promoting and Networking Collaboration: Systems thinking recognizes the value of networking and collaboration. It acknowledges that relationships, connections, and interactions with others influence careers. You can leverage systems thinking to build meaningful professional networks, engage in collaborative projects, and seek mentorship opportunities that enhance your career development. Overall, systems thinking provides a framework for understanding the complexity of career development and encourages you to approach your career with a more comprehensive and strategic mindset. By considering the interconnectedness of various elements and taking a long-term perspective, you can make informed decisions, adapt to change, and navigate your career more effectively.

Eleven

Culture

"Your work is going to fill a large part of your life, and the only way to be truly satisfied is to do what you believe is great work. And the only way to do great work is to love what you do. If you haven't found it yet, keep looking. Don't settle. As with all matters of the heart, you'll know when you find it." — Steve Jobs

Once your self-awareness is strong and you know your values, likes, and dislikes, then you will be more knowledgeable about the culture of the environment that you want to be in. It would be best if you gained an understanding of the culture of your industry of choice. Furthermore, it is just as critical that you are aware of the culture of the companies that you are interested in working. I cannot emphasize how important it is to find out as much as possible about the culture of the industry, company, or entrepreneurial endeavor you plan to create.

Culture is the implicit environment of an organization. Culture influences behaviors, norms, and attitudes within an organization. Cultural norms stipulate what is encouraged, discouraged, accepted, or rejected within different organizational areas. Culture develops through the combined experiences, values, and assumptions employees hold. A company's culture can be understood by observing the behaviors of its leaders and employees. Don't take culture for granted! Culture plays a significant role when changing careers as it can impact the transition process and overall success in the new career. Here's why culture is influential:

Industry-Specific Culture: Different industries have unique cultures, norms, and expectations. Understanding and adapting to the culture of the industry you're transitioning into is crucial for fitting in, building relationships, and navigating the new professional environment. Familiarize yourself with industry-specific practices, values, and communication styles to ensure a smoother career transition.

Company Culture: Each organization's distinct culture influences its values, work environment, and employee expectations. When changing careers, it is vital to research and assess the company culture of potential employers. A good fit with the company's culture can enhance job satisfaction, collaboration, and overall career fulfillment. Look for organizations whose culture aligns with your values and work style.

Networking and Relationships: Culture plays a vital role in networking and building professional relationships. Networking within the industry or field you're transitioning into allows you to connect with like-minded professionals, gain insights, and access new opportunities. Understanding and respecting the cultural norms of professional networking events, online communities, and mentorship programs can help you build effective relationships and expand your career network.

Adaptability and Integration: Changing careers often involves adapting to a new work environment, team dynamics, and organizational practices. Being aware of the cultural nuances and adapting to them can facilitate a smoother integration into the new role. Demonstrating openness, flexibility, and a willingness to learn can help you navigate cultural differences and establish credibility in your new career.

Professional Branding: Culture influences how you perceive and evaluate professional branding. When changing careers, aligning your brand with the cultural expectations of your target industry or profession is important. This includes crafting a resume, online presence, and personal narrative that resonate with the cultural values and requirements of the new career path.

Professional Development and Growth: Culture can shape professional development and growth opportunities within an industry or organization. Understanding the cultural norms and expectations around skill development, continuing education, and advancement can guide your career planning and help you identify the resources and avenues for growth in your new career.

Considering the cultural aspects of a career change ensures you are well-prepared to navigate the new environment, build meaningful relationships, and integrate effectively into the professional community. Awareness of cultural nuances enhances your adaptability, credibility, and long-term success in the new career.

Eleven — Culture

Cultural themes come in many layers. As you research industries, remember that each industry has its own implicit culture. For example, the finance, technology, and education industries have very different cultural norms. Many of these norms have been passed down for centuries, and many of them are new. Millennial entrepreneurs, successful or not, usually start companies with cultures based on flexible schedules, creativity, laidback dress codes, collaboration, and being highly motivated by purpose. It would help if you asked companies you interview about the company culture, particularly in the department you will be assigned. Examples of cultural elements are:

- How are new ideas received?
- What amenities are available for employees?
- How is information communicated?
- Do the leaders lead by example?
- How are new employees viewed?
- How are mistakes perceived?
- What information is shared and with whom?
- How do teams interact with one another?
- How are customers treated?
- What behaviors get you promoted?

Thousands of companies have excellent reputations externally, yet unfortunately, it's not until you work for them or a specific department do you see the proper attitudes and behaviors. When your values, drives, and needs align with your work environment, culture can unleash enormous energy toward a shared purpose, meaning, and successful career.

I had the pleasure of working for a fantastic utility for eight years. I had never worked for a utility prior, and I needed to learn the culture, but I needed to gain the skills needed to do the posted job. I remember like it was yesterday, how awkward I felt when I began working there. The average age was 45, almost 75% were white males, the average time of employment was 28 years, and it was very conservative. My first supervisor was not comfortable with African Americans.

I immediately realized that I was hired because the role (supplier diversity) required meeting, negotiating, and advocating for minority businesses, so it was perfect for an African American. Although getting acclimated to working at the utility was difficult, I did enjoy my work, and some of my colleagues are still close friends to this day.

As stated, culture is the implicit environment of an organization. When there is a good culture fit, you love what you do and are excited to come to work every morning. You want to see the company grow and actively contribute to that growth. Although I cared for most of my colleagues and made an excellent salary, I always needed to fit into the culture. I saw value in my work but never felt a sense of purpose or passion for growing in the company. I didn't feel a solid connection to the utility industry. Once I came to terms with my purpose, I pursued a career in education, and it has been one of the best decisions I have ever made.

Twelve

Resources

Websites for Success

The resources below will provide you with a plethora of insight and knowledge.

ionlearning.com - Online courses done in peer-learning groups

LinkedIn.com - Create a strong professional network

coursera.org - Take the world's best courses online

www.edx.org - Online Course from top Universities

harvardx.harvard.edu - Online courses, research, blog

www.futurelearn.com - Online courses

https://www.bls.gov/audience/jobseekers.htm - Bureau of Labor Statistics

http://www.hoovers.com - Industry analyses and company profiles

khanacademy.org - Tutoring and learning on just about everything

http://www.iftf.org/home/ - Institute for the Future (IFTF) brings people together to make the future, today.

https://www.mindtools.com - Career tools

https://www.nationalservice.gov - Nonprofit work opportunities

Career Inspiration TED Talks

TED is a media organization that posts motivational and knowledge-based talks online, under the slogan "ideas worth spreading". Here are some inspiring TED Talks that can provide motivation and insights for going through a career change:

- "Why Some of Us Don't Have One True Calling" by Emilie Wapnick: This talk challenges the notion of having a single, fixed career path and encourages embracing the concept of being a "multipotentiality" with diverse interests and talents.

- "How to Find Work You Love" by Scott Dinsmore: In this talk, Scott Dinsmore shares his journey of finding work that is meaningful and fulfilling. He provides practical advice on discovering your passions and aligning your career choices with your values.

- "The Power of Believing That You Can Improve" by Carol Dweck: Carol Dweck discusses the concept of a growth mindset, emphasizing the importance of believing in your ability to develop skills and overcome challenges during a career transition.

- "Why You Will Fail to Have a Great Career" by Larry Smith: In this humorous talk, economist Larry Smith highlights the common excuses and fears that hold people back from pursuing their dream careers. He challenges listeners to take risks and pursue their passions.

- "The Career Advice You Probably Didn't Get" by Susan Colantuono: Susan Colantuono addresses the lack of career advice focused on leadership and strategic skills. She emphasizes the importance of developing these skills to advance in your career and make an impact.

- "How to Make Hard Choices" by Ruth Chang: Ruth Chang explores the process of making difficult decisions, such as career changes. She emphasizes the power of embracing uncertainty and making choices that align with your values and sense of identity.

- "Why Some of Us Don't Have a True Calling" by Elizabeth Gilbert: Elizabeth Gilbert, the author of "Eat, Pray, Love," shares her perspective on finding passion and purpose in multiple areas of life. She encourages individuals to follow their curiosity and explore different paths.

These TED Talks offer valuable insights, stories, and perspectives to inspire individuals going through a career change. They can provide the encouragement and mindset shifts needed to navigate the challenges and embrace new opportunities.

Motivational TED Talks

- Tita Gray - My Greatest Fears Created My Strongest Values. https://www.youtube.com/watch?v=tmIiyC9n1eU

- Amy Cuddy - Your body language may shape who you are. www.ted.com/talks/amy_cuddy_your_body_language_shapes_who_you_are

- Simon Sinek - How great leaders inspire action. www.ted.com/talks/simon_sinek_how_great_leaders_inspire_action

- Brené Brown - The power of vulnerability. www.ted.com/talks/brene_brown_on_vulnerability

- Julian Treasure - How to speak so that people listen. www.ted.com/talks/julian_treasure_how_to_speak_so_that_people_want_to_listen

- Dan Pink - The Puzzle of Motivation. www.youtube.com/watch?v=rrkrvAUbU9Y

- Drew Dudley - Everyday Leadership. www.ted.com/talks/drew_dudley_everyday_leadership

These TED Talks offer valuable insights, stories, and perspectives to motivate your personal growth.

Podcasts

Here are some suggested podcasts that cater to women in career change and offer valuable insights, inspiration, and practical advice.

- "The New Corner Office" by Laura Vanderkam: This podcast explores strategies for managing time, productivity, and work-life balance. It provides practical tips and advice for professionals seeking to make the most of their careers.

- "Second Life" by Hillary Kerr: This podcast features interviews with successful women who have made significant career changes or found new paths of purpose and fulfillment. It offers inspiring stories and valuable insights for women seeking to navigate their own career transitions.

- "Happen to Your Career" by Scott Anthony Barlow: This podcast provides guidance and support for individuals looking to find work they love and make successful career transitions. It features interviews with experts and professionals who share their stories and practical tips.

- "The Career Relaunch Podcast" by Joseph Liu: This podcast explores stories of professionals who have successfully relaunched their careers. It provides insights, strategies, and inspiration for women seeking to make meaningful career changes.

- "Women at Work" by Harvard Business Review: This podcast focuses on the experiences, challenges, and opportunities women face in the workplace. It offers practical advice, research-based insights, and inspiring stories to empower women in their careers.

- "Bossed Up" by Emilie Aries: This podcast aims to empower women in their personal and professional lives. It covers topics such as career advancement, work-life balance, negotiation, and self-care, offering practical tips and advice for navigating career changes.

- "Career Contessa" by Career Contessa: This podcast explores various aspects of career development and provides insights and advice for women looking to advance their careers or make career changes. It features interviews with professionals from diverse industries.

- "The Tim Ferriss Show" by Tim Ferriss: While not exclusively focused on women, this podcast features interviews with high-performing individuals from various fields. It provides valuable insights into their strategies, habits, and experiences, which can inspire and inform career transitions.

Remember to explore different episodes within these podcasts to find the ones most relevant to your career change journey. Each podcast offers unique perspectives and stories that can help you gain valuable insights and navigate your own career transition successfully.

Suggested Reading

- The 5 Second Rule - Transform Your Life, Work, and Confidence with Everyday Courage.

- The Secret – This is a great book for learning the importance of changing how you think.

- The Mindset – This book makes you evaluate yourself based on two mindsets – the fixed mindset and the growth mindset.

- Outliers – This is one of the most compelling books of stories of success that I have ever read. This is about people that do things that are out of the ordinary.

- Non Violent Communication - NVC is based on the idea that all human beings have the capacity for compassion and only resort to violence or behavior that harms others when they don't recognize more effective strategies for meeting needs.

- The Wisdom of Crowds – This book demonstrates that under most circumstances, groups are remarkably intelligent and are often smarter than the smartest people in them.

- Thinking, Fast and Slow - The basic idea is simple there are two routes to persuasion, based on two basic modes of thinking, intuitive and rational.

- The Four Agreements - Rooted in traditional Toltec wisdom beliefs, four agreements in life are essential steps on the path to personal freedom.

- You Are a Badass - How to Stop Doubting Your Greatness and Start Living an Awesome Life.

- The Power of Habit - Why We Do What We Do in Life and Business

- Finding Flow – This book will describe ideas on living life to the fullest without wasting time and potential.

- The 7 Habits of Highly Successful People – You can never go wrong with a Stephen Covey classic. This book provides life lessons that are everyday affirmations.

- Who Moved My Cheese? - The text describes changing one's work and life, and four typical reactions to those changes.
- Start with Why - How great leaders inspire everyone to take action.

Blogs

These blog topics cover various aspects of a career change, including self-discovery, overcoming challenges, networking, skill development, and personal branding. Each topic provides an opportunity to delve deeper into the subject matter, share practical advice, and provide real-life examples and stories that resonate with readers.

- "Unleashing Your Potential: How to Identify and Harness Your Unique Talents"
- "Embracing the Unknown: Navigating the Challenges of Career Change with Confidence"
- "From Fear to Fearless: Overcoming Doubts and Taking the Leap into a New Career"
- "Discovering Your Passion: Unveiling What Truly Ignites Your Career Path"
- "The Power of Networking: Building Connections for Successful Career Transitions"
- "Resilience in the Face of Adversity: Stories of Career Change Triumphs"
- "Skills for the Future: Adapting and Thriving in an Evolving Job Market"
- "Career Reinvention at Midlife: Redefining Success and Finding Fulfillment"
- "Crafting Your Personal Brand: Strategies for Standing Out in a Competitive Job Market"
- "Leveraging Technology: Embracing Digital Tools and Platforms for Career Success"

Thirteen
Top Industries

An industry is a category that refers to groups of companies associated based on their primary business activity. As you research industries, remember that specific industries are more prevalent in particular locations. For example:

- Computers and electronics manufacturing industry - California

- Tourism and hospitality industry - California and Florida

- Ambulatory health care services industry - Alabama and Arkansas,

- Oil and gas extraction industry - Alaska and Colorado,

- Insurance industry - Connecticut, Delaware, and Illinois,

- Broadcasting and telecommunications industry - Georgia, New York, and Pennsylvania

- Accommodation industry - Hawaii and Nevada

- Chemical products manufacturing industry - Indiana and North Carolina

- Petroleum and coal products manufacturing industry - Louisiana

- Hospitals and nursing and residential care facilities industry - Maine and Massachusetts

- Federal Reserve banks and credit services - New York and South Dakota

- Publishing industries, except internet (includes software) - Washington State

According to research some of the top industries for 2017 are listed below along with an extensive listing of national and global industries.

Green Construction	Veterinary Technology
Health Care	Physical Therapy
Automation	Franchising
Biomedical Engineering	Education and Training
Tourism	

Alphabetical Listing of Industries

The list below shows all the industries, sectors, and categories that are profiled in this section.

Abortion Policy/Anti-Abortion
Abortion Policy/Pro-Abortion Rights
Accountants
Advertising/Public Relations
Aerospace, Defense Contractors
Agribusiness
Agricultural Services & Products
Agriculture
Air Transport
Air Transport Unions
Airlines
Alcoholic Beverages
Alternative Energy Production & Services
Architectural Services
Attorneys/Law Firms
Auto Dealers
Auto Manufacturers
Automotive

Banking, Mortgage
Banks, Commercial
Banks, Savings & Loans
Bars & Restaurants
Beer, Wine & Liquor
Books, Magazines & Newspapers

Broadcasters, Radio/TV
Builders/General Contractors
Builders/Residential
Building Materials & Equipment
Building Trade Unions
Business Associations
Business Services

Cable & Satellite TV Production & Distribution
Car Dealers
Car Dealers, Imports
Car Manufacturers
Casinos / Gambling
Cattle Ranchers/Livestock
Chemical & Related Manufacturing
Chiropractors
Civil Servants/Public Officials
Clergy & Religious Organizations
Clothing Manufacturing
Coal Mining
Colleges, Universities & Schools
Commercial Banks
Commercial TV & Radio Stations
Communications/Electronics
Computer Software

Conservative/Republican
Construction
Construction Services
Construction Unions
Credit Unions
Crop Production & Basic Processing
Cruise Lines
Cruise Ships & Lines

Dairy
Defense
Defense Aerospace
Defense Electronics
Defense/Foreign Policy Advocates
Dentists
Doctors & Other Health Professionals
Drug Manufacturers

Education
Electric Utilities
Electronics Manufacturing & Equipment
Electronics, Defense Contractors
Energy & Natural Resources
Entertainment Industry
Environmental

Farm Bureaus
Farming
Finance/Credit Companies
Finance, Insurance & Real Estate
Food & Beverage
Food Processing & Sales
Food Products Manufacturing
Food Stores
For-profit Education
For-profit Prisons
Foreign & Defense Policy
Forestry & Forest Products

Foundations, Philanthropists & Non-Profits
Funeral Services

Gambling & Casinos
Gambling, Indian Casinos
Garbage Collection/Waste Management
Gas & Oil
Gay & Lesbian Rights & Issues
General Contractors
Government Employee Unions
Government Employees
Gun Control
Gun Rights

Health
Health Professionals
Health Services/HMOs
Hedge Funds
HMOs & Health Care Services
Home Builders
Hospitals & Nursing Homes
Hotels, Motels & Tourism
Human Rights

Ideological/Single-Issue
Indian Gaming
Industrial Unions
Insurance
Internet

Labor
Lawyers & Lobbyists
Lawyers / Law Firms
Leadership PACs
Liquor, Wine & Beer
Livestock
Lobbyists
Lodging / Tourism
Logging, Timber & Paper Mills

Manufacturing, Misc
Marine Transport
Meat processing & products
Medical Supplies
Mining
Misc Manufacturing & Distributing
Misc Unions
Miscellaneous Defense
Miscellaneous Services
Mortgage Bankers & Brokers
Motion Picture Production & Distribution
Music Production

Natural Gas Pipelines
Newspaper, Magazine & Book Publishing
Non-profits, Foundations & Philanthropists
Nurses
Nursing Homes/Hospitals
Nutritional & Dietary Supplements

Oil & Gas
Other

Payday Lenders
Pharmaceutical Manufacturing
Pharmaceuticals / Health Products
Philanthropy
Phone Companies
Physicians & Other Health Professionals
Politics
Postal Unions
Poultry & Eggs
Power Utilities
Printing & Publishing
Private Equity & Investment Firms

Professional Sports, Sports Arenas & Related Equipment & Services
Public Employees
Public Sector Unions
Publishing & Printing

Radio/TV Stations
Railroads
Real Estate
Record Companies/Singers
Recorded Music & Music Production
Recreation /Live Entertainment
Religious Organizations/Clergy
Residential Construction
Restaurants & Drinking Establishments
Retail Sales
Retired

Savings & Loans
Schools/Education
Sea Transport
Securities & Investment
Special Trade Contractors
Sports, Professional
Steel Production
Stock Brokers/Investment Industry
Student Loan Companies
Sugar Cane & Sugar Beets

Teachers Unions
Teachers/Education
Telecom Services & Equipment
Telephone Utilities
Textiles
Timber, Logging & Paper Mills
Tobacco
Transportation
Transportation Unions

Trash Collection/Waste
   Management
Trucking
TV / Movies / Music
TV Production

Unions
Unions, Airline
Unions, Building Trades
Unions, Industrial
Unions, Misc
Unions, Public Sector
Unions, Teacher
Unions, Transportation
Universities, Colleges & Schools

Vegetables & Fruits
Venture Capital

Waste Management
Wine, Beer & Liquor
Women's Issues

Fourteen
Conclusion

We all have a journey to trek that I call the rollercoaster of life. You usually do not know what to expect, but you strap in and know you will eventually reach a destination. There isn't one best practice for pursuing your career, but having a better understanding of yourself is one thing you have complete control over. How you think, how you study, how you pray, how you meditate, your choice of friends, what you eat, etc., are things that you can control, and they are all necessary as you decide how your journey will flow. Gandhi said,

> *"your beliefs become your thoughts,*
> *your thoughts become your words,*
> *your words become your actions,*
> *your actions become your habits,*
> *your habits become your values,*
> *your values become your destiny."*

As you learn whom you want to become in your transformation and what you want to practice, remember that you are perfect and imperfect, just as you are. You are unique for a reason, and the universe is waiting for your contributions to improve this world. One of the best ways to do that is by enjoying the things you do in life to the fullest. You will be challenged, you will be hurt (decide on who is worth being hurt by), you will be disappointed, you will make mistakes, and you will be judged. Remember that you are important and worthy of success.

Keep people around you who make you laugh, inspire, love, and will be there to pick you up when you fall. Handling criticism, disappointment, and failure is crucial when navigating a career transition. It would be best if you adopted a growth mindset, which involves viewing challenges as opportunities for growth and learning. Instead of seeing criticism, disappointment, or failure as setbacks, see them as valuable feedback that can help you improve and adjust your approach. Embrace a mindset that recognizes failure as a stepping stone toward success. Make sure to practice self-love. Be kind and compassionate to yourself when faced with criticism, disappointment, or failure. Understand that setbacks are a natural part of any career transition, and everyone experiences them. Treat yourself with understanding, forgiveness, and patience. Remind yourself that setbacks are setups to define your worth or potential. Instead of viewing criticism as unfavorable, seek constructive feedback from trusted mentors, colleagues, or professionals in your new career field. Listen actively, be open to suggestions, and use the feedback to improve your skills, knowledge, and approach. Constructive feedback can provide valuable insights and help you make necessary adjustments in your career transition.

When facing disappointment, reframe the situation by focusing on the opportunities it presents. Look for alternative paths, explore different options, and consider how setbacks can lead to new possibilities. Disappointment can often be a catalyst for positive change and growth. Failure is an inevitable part of any career transition. Instead of letting it discourage you, use failure as a learning opportunity. Analyze what went wrong, identify lessons learned, and determine how you can apply those lessons moving forward. Embrace a mindset that sees failure as a stepping stone to success and a chance to develop resilience and perseverance.

Most importantly, self-care is essential during criticism, disappointment, and failure. Engage in activities that help you recharge, relax, and maintain a positive mindset. This may include exercise, meditation, spending time with loved ones, pursuing hobbies, or seeking professional support. Remember, career transitions are rarely linear, and setbacks are a natural part of the process. How you respond to criticism, disappointment, and failure can ultimately shape your career trajectory. By adopting a growth mindset, seeking feedback, and maintaining self-compassion, you can navigate these challenges and continue moving forward on your career transition journey.

There are several pathways to fulfillment; find yours. Is it working for others, being an entrepreneur, working from home, or being a stay-at-home parent? All are great ways to live, and they are all interchangeable. You don't have to aspire to one career; go after as many as you want. Just have a purpose and meaning behind what you are doing. We spend much of our lives at work, significantly affecting our well-being. This is why choosing a career is something that you shouldn't take lightly. It's important to examine all the options available before making a final decision, as this will help ensure your future professional happiness and security. Determining the right industry helps you zero in on the ideal career, which minimizes the risk of making a wrong decision. By looking at the industries rather than individual professions, you can also identify the fastest-growing industries, which can help you change careers easier.

According to a forecast from the Institute for the Future (IFTF), 85% of the jobs in 2030 have yet to be invented (These Are the Jobs Everyone Will Compete for In the Future | Money. https://money.com/6-future-jobs/). Ten years after that, the workforce may be unrecognizable. So how do you choose the right industry, whether to work for a company or become an entrepreneur? You think about all of the things that you like or that intrigue you. Automation will be a massive trend in the coming years. Do you love teaching, guiding, and influencing others? Do you love cars and everything about automobiles? Are you intrigued by the stock and financial markets? Do you want to start a business in a particular industry? Is your motivation to make a difference in the world? Do you want to make a difference in health care? Do you want to make a difference in how animals are treated? Do you want to change labor laws or human trafficking? Think like an entrepreneur! To start a business, you should research the market thoroughly, understand the product or service in-depth, and understand staffing needs. This is how you should proceed in knowing your path. When you approach knowing the industry like this, you will excel in your process.

Although it is critical to know your purpose, passion, knowledge, and personality, it is just as important to be informed about every aspect of the journey that you are interested. By focusing on the journey, you cultivate mindfulness and an appreciation for the present moment. Instead of constantly chasing future goals, you learn to savor the experiences, lessons, and growth that occur along the way. This allows you to find joy and fulfillment in the process itself, rather than solely relying on achieving a specific outcome. The journey is a transformative process that fosters personal growth and self-discovery. It provides opportunities to learn new skills, gain valuable experiences, and develop resilience and adaptability. Each step of the journey contributes to your personal and professional development, shaping whom you become along the way.

When you focus on the journey, you give yourself permission to enjoy the process rather than constantly striving for the next milestone. It allows you to celebrate small wins, find fulfillment in everyday tasks, and experience a sense of satisfaction and progress throughout your career journey. Being too fixated on a specific destination can limit your ability to recognize and embrace unexpected opportunities that arise along the way. By focusing on the journey, you remain open, adaptable, and responsive to new possibilities. This flexibility allows you to make course corrections, explore different paths, and seize opportunities that may lead to even greater fulfillment and success. The journey is not solely about career achievements, but also about maintaining overall well-being and work-life balance. By focusing on the journey, you prioritize self-care, relationships, and personal fulfillment alongside your professional goals. This holistic approach leads to a more sustainable and fulfilling career experience.

The journey of life and career is like a rollercoaster, full of ups and downs, unexpected twists, and moments of exhilaration and uncertainty. It's important to acknowledge that everyone's journey is unique, and there isn't a one-size-fits-all approach to pursuing a career. Understanding oneself is a fundamental aspect of navigating the career journey. Knowing your values, interests, strengths, and goals can provide a strong foundation for decision-making and help you align your choices with your authentic self. Taking control of your thoughts, actions, and habits can have a significant impact on your career path and overall well-being.

Self-reflection, continuous learning, and personal development are key elements in shaping your journey. Engaging in practices like studying, praying, meditating, and surrounding yourself with positive influences can foster self-awareness, clarity, and resilience. Building a supportive network of friends and mentors who inspire and challenge you can also play a crucial role in your career exploration and growth. Additionally, taking care of your physical and mental well-being is vital. Paying attention to what you eat, engaging in regular exercise, and practicing self-care can contribute to your overall energy, focus, and motivation.

It's important to remember that the journey of a career is not a linear path, and there may be detours and unexpected turns along the way. Embrace the process, stay open to new opportunities, and be willing to adapt and learn from each experience. Ultimately, your career journey is about discovering and creating a life that aligns with your passions, values, and aspirations. Embrace the choices and control you have, and trust that with self-awareness, perseverance, and a positive mindset, you can navigate the rollercoaster of life and create a fulfilling career path.

While having goals and aspirations is essential, the journey shapes your character, enriches your experiences, and contributes to your overall happiness and well-being. By embracing and appreciating the journey, you can find meaning and fulfillment throughout your career, regardless of whether you reach a specific destination. Believe in yourself, embrace a challenge, step out of your comfort zone, and most importantly enjoy your life. You only get one.

www.ingramcontent.com/pod-product-compliance
Lightning Source LLC
Chambersburg PA
CBHW050820090426

42737CB00021B/3451